Leading Wise

Leading Wise

INSPIRATIONAL REFLECTIONS
FOR CORPORATE LEADERS

EBONI ADAMS MONK

Pickled Roots Publishing

Copyright © 2021 by Eboni Adams Monk.

All rights reserved.

No part of this publication may be reproduced, in whole or in part, stored in or introduced into a retrieval system, or transmitted, in any form or by any means (electronic, mechanical, photocopying, recording, or otherwise), without the express written permission of the publisher.

Published by Pickled Roots Publishing, Ellicott City
www.pickledroots.com

Cover design: Kozakura

ISBN: 978-1-7346124-4-8

DEDICATION

I dedicate this book to the Elders of traditional cultural communities around the world. May the light that dances in your hearts be grounded in the fabric of the Earth and blossom like roses eternal.

CONTENTS

Preface	13
Reflection	19
Power	23
Purpose	39
Community	55
Tradition	69
And So It Is	85
My Reflections	87

PREFACE

Because of my Ancestors, I am. And for years, my connection to them, my lineage, my culture, and my something bigger than myself has been guiding me.

From the west coast of Africa, by way of the Delta portal, I am the daughter of those who served, comforted, and guided the community. I come from those who rise from deep soil to bridge the past and future. I am a leader. No matter where I go, I lead. I lead in the spirit of service, guided by the needs of those around me. I come from a long line of people with a rich history and propensity for leadership. I am humbled and inspired by the stories of grandmothers and grandfathers who reached beyond themselves to help and transform their community.

While some fail to see their power, I have been unable to dismiss it. So I followed my heart and sacred pathways and embraced the wisdom traditions of my lineage. Along the way, I received messages, signs, and confirmation that I was on the right path.

But the path wasn't always comfortable for me.

An artist at heart, I enjoy spending my days writing poetry and singing among the trees. But in America I was ushered into corporate life, where my love of science and math propelled me to join the ranks of engineers. Even in the corporate environment, my African roots were always with me. I quickly understood that the corporate world was a microcosm of the larger world. Often, however, I was the only woman or the only African American person in the room. So it is no surprise that my time with the Elders of various African, Native American, and Hindu communities provided a foundation for me to grow and thrive—personally and at work.

Today, I am a corporate leader, leading from the same spirit of service that my Elders instilled in me. Although I longed to spend months at a time abroad studying at their feet, for the past twenty-five years I learned from my Elders in practical ways. I learned during vacations in Bahia studying with powerful Elders of West African Orisha culture. I learned while engaged in deeply personal and transformational healing work with a Warrior Woman representing the mystic Hindu tradition. Finally, I learned during weekend visits with Native American Choctaw Elders and weekends spent practicing yoga philosophies and asanas, followed by plenty of contemplation. Through these experiences, I realized their teachings were rooted in similar values and connected by a universal thread of truth. I used these truths to develop a philosophy that would shape my perspective on life, especially my life at work. I came to understand that it is our life experiences that shape us and initiate us into a higher level of conscious living.

And then one day, I looked up and realized that I had actually gained the wisdom I needed to thrive through my life experiences. The challenges and victories of everyday life had tested my ability to understand and deepen the lessons I had learned with the Elders. Those challenges shaped me. I am forever grateful for the wisdom that has been imparted to me. And I am compelled to share what I have learned. Why? To encourage others to lead in a soul-inspired way and to preserve and uplift the wisdom of ancient Earth.

Although many of us separate our personal and professional lives, they are actually one and the same. My Elders taught me the essence of culture, leadership, and community within a traditional community context. In these communities we are guided by the wisdom of our Ancestors. I learned from sacred texts, oral traditions, and sacred ceremony and then interpreted the lessons to guide my beliefs, thoughts, and actions in situations I encountered in life, including work. Since corporations are cultural microcosms, the same foundational philosophies regarding leadership and community I learned in traditional indigenous communities also apply to the workplace. I believe work offers a sacred path we can travel to help us learn more about ourselves and others. As a result, I approach my work with a sense of respect for the possibility that an opportunity to transform myself or my teams may open up at any moment.

There is a Congolese proverb about leadership that says, "If you are a leader, be like the moon, not like the sun." This saying gets to the heart of why this book is necessary. Unlike the sun, the moon shines in the dark of night, lighting the way when it is most needed. In relation to leadership, the symbolism of the moon is related to the reflection required to lead, one's ability to adapt to situations and people, and the process of becoming enlightened. This holistic approach to leadership provides a path to the results needed for leaders to be successful, albeit in a different way than typical leadership training.

This book is a compilation of my insights, combining my fondness for natural poetic inquiry with inspirational guidance for leaders. It offers that perhaps corporate life can be poetic, healing, and transformational, like the characteristics of the moon. And as leaders, if we shift to lead from this place of transformation, perhaps our work will be more successful, meaningful, and offer more fulfilment.

This book is an offering to the corporate women and men who are struggling to balance their grand purpose with their everyday lives, which are often consumed by work. This is a book for those who know they are worth more than the work they do every day at their jobs. This is a book for those who have lost the inner spark and excitement for leading. Finally, this book is for those who feel the pull from deep inside themselves to contribute to the world more mindfully, powerfully, and completely. May your purpose be supported by community. May your community be strengthened by tradition. May you wrap yourself in tradition and let your power unfold.

REFLECTION

Reviewing. Thinking. Meditating. Observing. Pondering. Daydreaming. These are all words that exemplify reflection. Yet these words offer only clues because none of them have the power signified by the word *reflection*. When we reflect, we remember or recall with the intention of receiving clarity, meaning, and, perhaps, enlightenment. When we reflect, we take in a moment and bring it into the core of ourselves for guidance. When we reflect, we signal to ourselves that we are open to shift our perspectives. When we reflect, we say that we are willing to not only listen but to hear the inner wisdom deep inside us.

Reflection opens up pathways for us to connect with our own innate wisdom. The moon, which is a symbol of deep mystery and inner knowing, reflects the sun's light but also gives greater meaning to the sun's power. As such, the moon herself becomes a great symbol of the power of reflection.

Reflection is about seeing ourselves in the mirror. It requires us to look into the mirror and explore ourselves to find wisdom and insight. Reflection requires us to step into honesty. It requires us to step into any resistance that may appear. Reflection invites us when we are leading our everyday lives. It is there when we step outside. It is there in our failures. It is there in our greatness.

The reflections in this book are intended to inspire you to reflect on your philosophy and demonstration of leadership. The act of reflection is a very personal process. I invite you to carve out space for reflection in your own way. Begin your workday with reflection. End your day with reflection. Honor each reflection with deep breath. Honor each reflection with stillness. Move with the spirit of each reflection as you move through your day. Observe how the words impact you as you go about your everyday life. Listen to your intuition. What message does each reflection have for you? How does each reflection touch you? How are you moved? How can you show up differently as a leader? And how does your leadership invite you to grow on a personal level?

Your reflections may guide you to lead differently. They may challenge your beliefs. But, always, reflection is a gift that unfolds. It shows us the way, makes us whole, and carries us home to ourselves.

There is power in nature and in the breath of life. You will only find power when you surrender to the balance that exists at the core of your heart.

INSPIRED BY KALI MAIE,
TEACHER, VISIONARY, AND HEALER

POWER

Words have been written to define what power is. The descriptions invoke images in our minds. But power is also felt. Power can be mysterious. Some people don't realize they have it. Other people actively seek out power. How it shows up for us is unique to each one of us. Our response to power depends on our experiences with power. When you feel it, you know what power is. When you dare to grow, when you dare to show up, the spirit of power is near. When you shift the course of events, when you inspire, the spirit of power is near. When you offer guidance, when you are decisive, the spirit of power is near. When you change minds, including your own, the spirit of power is near. Power does not belong only to the leaders of our organizations. It ripples throughout the entire organization, touching all who come into contact with it.

How can the ageless view of power influence your leadership? What is your relationship to power? Do you crave it? Are you fearful of it? How do you use the power you have? Are you intentional with your use of power? How do you lift others up? What is your responsibility to the spirit of power? And what if the purpose of power is to shake us to our core, revealing something new?

TRUE POWER COMES FROM WITHIN.

At the intersection of our passions, talents, and deep wisdom lies the seed of power. From that seed, true power blossoms into a force that transforms the self and positively impacts communities. True power aspires to greatness. It inspires. It stirs the soul. It shifts hearts and minds.

Power must be nurtured and honored. In traditional wisdom communities, Elders train leaders to step with honor into the power of serving the community. This journey requires openness to receive guidance and surrender to the needs of the community.

Power requires responsibility. It demands accountability. When one is called to step into a place of power, that power has been entrusted for safekeeping.

GIVE THANKS.
YOUR POWER IS A
GIFT.

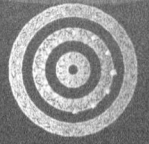

The gift of leadership is a rite of passage into the action of guiding the minds, spirits, hearts, and souls of those entrusted to us to lead. As leaders, we hold space for our teams and communities to grow. We nurture. We guide. It is an honor.

UNBROKEN CIRCLES

MAKE WAY

FOR WHYS TO INSPIRE
UNSEEN FLAMES INSIDE
TO LIGHT THE WAY.

Power empowers. It is too grand to keep bound. It moves, seeking an opportunity to shapeshift. As leaders, we must approach power reverently. We must use it consciously. And then offer its gifts to the world.

YOU
INVITE ME TO
UNEARTH ALL OF ME
AND LEAVE ME IN
AWE.

In all things exists the power of transformation. Surrender and humility make the way possible, unveiling an unexpected yet inevitable path. Gifted with the chance to learn about ourselves more deeply opens up even more power to us. The cycle becomes even more powerful when we deepen our perspective and evolve our leadership in ways that teach and inspire others.

Leaders are because communities are. Communities are because people are. People are because they are alive with purpose and passion and feeling, enlivening the Earth with promise. How will you lead?

Each person has a purpose and mission in life. We live on Earth to learn things. During our life on Earth, we should recognize and find out what our mission is because when we find our mission, we can act correctly in accordance to love, peace, harmony, charity, and solidarity.

— IYALORISHA MARCIA DE OGUM
OF ILÊ AXÉ EWÁ OLODUMARE AND
COUNSELOR OF CULTURAL POLITICS

PURPOSE

I can hear the Elders say "in all things is a purpose." The idea that there is a force or power behind people and events is a common belief among indigenous communities. Purpose is the reason something exists. It is our why. Each of us has a purpose—a reason for being and doing. In their role as guides, the Elders can offer deep insights into the purpose of those in their communities.

Discovering purpose is the adventure of life itself. Our natural talents offer clues to our purpose. Our interests and deep passions offer even more clues. Where we find our beliefs are challenged offers insights to our purpose. Where we feel compelled to act in response to calls of need offers even more hints. Alignment with purpose allows us to use our talents and our energy efficiently to achieve our goals. Without purpose, we wander, seeking fulfillment for the soul. Knowing your purpose is powerful. Helping to guide others to their purpose is magic.

What is your purpose? What insights do your life experiences offer about your purpose? Are you living your purpose? What is your purpose as a leader? How does your role as a leader guide your purpose? Is your purpose aligned with your company's purpose? How can you use your leadership to guide others toward their purpose?

EVERY PURPOSE IS
SACRED.

SACRED IS OUR JOURNEY. LIKE TRUTH FLOWING IN ANCIENT RIVERS. IT IS ALL LIFE.

Life is a journey. There is a beginning. There is an evolution. Within the questioning, within the daily tasks, there is an energy that pulsates from within each of us. Called by many names in wisdom cultures, it is the purpose of our being that whispers from within.

I AWOKE.

AND THERE YOU WERE.
LOOKING AT MY SOUL
WITH MY EYES.

When something new is created, it is done with a purpose in mind. Babies are born accompanied by hopes and dreams. Teams are created to serve a goal. When there is creation, its purpose must be nurtured.

"AS ABOVE, SO BELOW."

Purpose manifests itself in the things we see. True purpose is born of desire and devotion to evolving. Tapping into true purpose is the deeper wisdom that is well understood and nourished by indigenous cultures.

Self-awareness is an important, yet often underdeveloped, skill. Without it, one can struggle to feel fulfilled. With it, one's purpose is made clear and becomes the foundation upon which decisions are made and life is lived fully.

WHAT CAN I SAY ABOUT
THIS THING CALLED
LIFE?

IT EXISTS.
SO WE EXIST.
WE LISTEN.
WE DO.
WE LEARN.

Work, being a part of life, also follows the wisdom of purpose. Companies are created to provide products and services to help others and generate abundance in its many forms. The creation of a company thereby affirms there is purpose. The company creates community and has the power to evolve all it comes into contact with. Companies create an environment for professional growth and development of their employees. In the spirit of wisdom traditions, companies must also create an environment for personal growth and development. In essence, we have the opportunity for deep learning as we work.

AS THE WATERS CARESS, I RISE FROM RIVERS UNSEEN.

WISDOM ROOTED IN THE EARTH, BRANCHING LIKE TREES.

FORGING A PATH ON AN UNKNOWN ROAD.

EVERYTHING AROUND ME FEEDS MY SOUL.

We are shaped by our environments. Our work environments create opportunities for us to learn about ourselves so we can grow and thrive. We offer our gifts. We learn to communicate. We learn to discern. We face challenges. We grow. And when we are aligned and self-aware, we express our purpose along the way.

EVERY PURPOSE IS
SACRED.

SHARED PURPOSE CAN BE MAGICAL.

Community makes us stronger, it reminds us that we are in this world together. The beloved community enables us to witness and engage the endless reflections of possibilities of the human race. Rich is our well of possibility when we release ourselves to a greater wholeness. We begin that process through self-awareness, truth telling, and deep listening.

— AUDRI SCOTT WILLIAMS, GLOBAL PEACE WALKER AND VISIONARY AUTHOR

COMMUNITY

There is power in community. Within community, surrounded by others, I have found support and wisdom. The wealth of experience that is shared within the community is an invaluable source of inspiration, insight, and support. The community is also a place where we are challenged to grow to our highest potential. In indigenous communities, the Elders teach the younger members of the community the culture and important lessons necessary for its members to succeed. The Elders set expectations for living. They are interested in balance of the body, mind, heart, and spirit.

Community holds us accountable to each other and the ideals of our community. Community allows us to express ourselves as individuals within the context of the broader community. We come together to pray, sing, dance, laugh, cry, and look into the hearts of each other. Here, we connect. Here, we develop good character. Here, we are whole. Such depth and purpose is the challenge from the spirit of community to our corporate communities.

How does your company support the ideal of community? What is the purpose of your work community? How do you connect with others? How do you support others to express their talents? How does your work community support each person's personal and professional growth? As a leader, how do you ensure purpose and the best interests of the community guide decisions?

WE FLOW AS ONE,
SHARING OUR MAGIC
WITH THE WORLD.

More than a gathering of people, community is the expression of shared purpose and values. Sacred space is created as we come together. Our commitment to gather strengthens our bond and uplifts every part of the community.

WE MOVE TOGETHER

AND I FEEL YOUR SOUL
COMMUNING
WITH MY OWN

Community is our collective soul's expression of who we are and who we aspire to be. Community is a relationship between individual perspectives, the community's culture, and our choice to align with others. Work is no exception.

THE OLD WOMEN GATHER TOGETHER THE DAY AND ALL ITS GLORY.

THEY CHANT SOFTLY. THEY SING ALOUD. FROM THEIR HANDS SPRINGS LIFE. AN ANCIENT MAGIC BROUGHT TO A NEW DAY.

FROM WOMEN WHO GATHER THE DAY TO GIVE PRAISE FOR THE UNIVERSE.

On a warm day in Bahia, Brazil, I observed the Elders. They were women with seasoned ability to transform potential to greatness. They sang and shared their experiences as they chopped onions and okra and boiled herbs. Their words stirred my heart although I did not logically understand the language. I was home, a place where my heart and soul was nurtured. Those women taught me the spirit of community and the importance traditions and culture play in the strength and longevity of community.

EVERY BUTTERFLY HAS
A STORY.

EVERY BIRD HAS A
SONG TO SING.

EVERY TREE HOLDS A
SECRET.

EVERY STAR
BRIGHTENS THE SKY.

AND THEN THERE IS
YOU.

The beauty of community lies in its people. Each one bringing talents and ideas to shape the whole.

IN THE SPACE WHERE COLORS MERGE, WE ARE MADE WHOLE.

The art of leadership is a leader's ability to serve an individual's purpose and talents and the community's mission and culture. Leaders coordinate, blend, and manage parts of the community to support the mission and the people. They make certain the community evolves while living and staying true to its purpose.

We share memories that connect the generations and remind us we are one. Tradition is the privilege of honoring those who taught us and dedicated their lives to us.

ADAMS AND HENRY FAMILY ELDERS

TRADITION

Tradition permeates the fabric of every community. Tradition ensures that cultural values, beliefs, and behaviors endure.

Tradition lives within the community. It is kept alive by the people who honor the practices of past generations. Within indigenous traditions, there are prescribed ways of communicating ancient wisdom, nurturing the community, and honoring the beliefs of the culture. There is meaning and symbolism in these time-honored and closely held traditions. The stewards of tradition are important members of the community. They ensure the community continues to grow. Through rites of passage, sacred ceremony, community gatherings, and apprenticeship, leaders are molded to serve the community and uphold the traditions. With the spirit of tradition, we honor the past while we move into the future. With the spirit of tradition, the community remains rooted to its purpose and power.

What are the values of your company? How are your company's values reinforced through your company's traditions? Who are the stewards of your community's traditions? As a leader, how do you adapt to current needs while honoring your strengths and authenticity?

ROOTED IN THE PAST
I AM
VISIONING THE
FUTURE.

The Sankofa symbol from Ghana teaches us that we must remember knowledge from the past to build upon its foundation of lessons and wisdom to create an abundant future. Tradition is the pathway through which ancient wisdom flows.

IN EACH MOMENT BE
PRESENT, AND
FIND THE SACRED.

This point in time is the connection between the past and the future. We honor our past by expressing our community's values in our behaviors and actions. We show the importance of the values by teaching and modeling to others. Continuous expression reseeds the community and allows the community to thrive.

LOOK IN THE MIRROR
TO SEE THE WISDOM OF
YOUR SOUL.

African Griots tell the history and stories of our community. They know the value is passing along wisdom that the community has learned through the generations. Preserving ancient wisdom allows the community to remember its achievements and heed the warnings signaled from past failures. The wisdom is there as a guide for illumination as we journey through each moment of our lives.

THE TRADITION OF WISDOM IS OUR FOUNDATION.

THE WISDOM OF TRADITION IS OUR POWER.

The sacred gathering spaces of indigenous communities are special places. Here, everyday life slows and the deep rhythm of the wholeness of life quickens. Gathered together in the spirit of the community, we become one. We are one. Each with our own roles, functions, and responsibilities, but one nonetheless. Together, we keep our tradition alive.

ALL THAT FLOWS
FROM ME FLOWS WITH
DEVOTION.

Without devotion, the work takes more than it gives. Working more than a few hours a day on anything requires discipline and a level of devotion. Without devotion, the work becomes a chore. And the soul is often lost.

Tradition invites us to honor it through our actions and support it through our work. When done with devotion, the work is exalted.

THE PATH IS ALWAYS
LOVE.

The energy of love is seeking us. It calls for us to salute it in everything that we do. With intention and power, our work can be an expression of love. The essence of the Greek word Meraki is the energy of loving your work so intensely that you leave a piece of your soul in your work. Work rooted in love blossoms for the world and sprinkles seeds that inspire others.

AND SO IT IS

Written in the fabric of traditional indigenous communities around the world are stories that inspire and cover us with wisdom. Whether proverb or fable, their power lies in their timelessness and unyielding observations about life. When we surrender to the flow of life our lives become filled with intentioned experiences, where we seek to consciously learn through each experience. We honor those experiences. We are grateful for them. We honor every way in which they show up for us, even as we go about our days working and relating inside of corporate environments. And perhaps one day our reflections will lead us to joy and success that fulfills the soul.

LEADER AFFIRMATION

Together, we honor the tradition of sacred learning where we pass on the jewels that make us who we are.

We honor the circle of leaders who stand with us.

May our devotion guide us. May we tell our stories. And watch them turn to magic.

May our leadership be offered in the spirit of service that we may guide our communities and teams to shine their light and dance in their purpose.

May our power flow from a place of surrender.

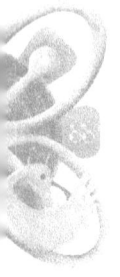

May we open to the adventure of work. May our ideas be born and become manifest from love, moving out into the world and touching all who cross its path.

May we dance the rite of passage into courageous leadership.

May we acknowledge the blessing that requires us to renew ourselves.

As all endings are beginnings, may we find our place among those who sing forth a new day for the Earth.

MY REFLECTIONS

Use the space below to record your reflections.

www.ingramcontent.com/pod-product-compliance
Lightning Source LLC
Chambersburg PA
CBHW071409080526
44587CB00017B/3225